Bedtime Poetry

A Sensual Collection

By Pamela Norris

Preparation for publishing, book cover, and poetry
By Pamela Norris

This book was printed in the United States of America

ISBN: 0615975682
ISBN-13: 978-0615975689

To order additional copies, contact:
http://www.createspace.com/4622989
Amazon.com
Pamela-Norris.com

Or
Email: Artsypoetry101@gmail.com

DEDICATION

This collection of poetry is dedicated to those who know and understand that sensuality and sexuality are a part of life. Always remember to speak your truth, and never stop giving yourselves permission to 'be'...

PAMELA NORRIS

CONTENTS

ACKNOWLEDGMENTS

To supporters of the arts, my fellow artists, and those who are open minded enough to read and enjoy this collection of poetry. Thank you for allowing me to share a part of my creativity with you.

DISCLAIMER

Let Me Be

I can be prim and proper to artsy and free spirited
I love them both and everything in between
Don't make me choose one way

Let me be

I don't want to get stuck being one way
I like the freedom of exploration
This enables me to create
Creativity does not take place when my spirit feels
confined

So please stop trying to lock me in by forcing me
into what you think I should be
Allow me to be who I am
Just as I allow you to be who you are
Without judgment...

Let me be

Pamela Norris

3 p.m.

My love has gone away on a journey
Oh how I miss him
I'm not sure when he is returning
But how I long to kiss his handsome face
And feel his muscular arms around my body

My days seem like time has slowed down
By night my heart echoes his name
In his absence my love has grown stronger
I have never known this feeling with any other

My love calls daily at 3p.m.
My ears burn with eagerness just to hear his voice
I close my eyes imagining that he is sitting next to me
That we are together and not connected by
An electronic device

He tells me how much he loves me
Then he asks me what I would do to him if he
Was with me now
I said, oh baby, wherever the moment takes us
After the many hugs and kisses upon your arrival
I would take you by the hand and lead you to our room
We would get naked under the covers while
Sipping hot chocolate
You can tell me all about your journey
As our hot bodies cuddle

Then I'll slip down under the covers
To tickle your navel with my tongue
Your manly rod is snuggled between my breasts

I squeeze them together and slide up and down
Uhm, can you feel it? I love to massage you this way
On my way down, the tip on my tongue hits the tip of
Your thick, hard manly rod
I let it slip into my mouth, oh you like that don't you?
My tongue swirls like chocolate does in vanilla ice
cream
Your body shakes like a moving fault line

But I don't stop there, I work my way up
I move in a slow motion until you penetrate the
Doorway of my treasure chest
It's so warm inside, oh so wet and ooo so tight
Work it out baby, work it
Now it's my turn to tremble like a moving fault line
Be very proud, you did this to me
I can't wait until you return home
I enjoy our love making by phone
But nothing is better than having you here
He said, "really? I'll be there soon, sweetie"

Just then, I heard a knock on the door
Hey baby, someone is at the door....hold on a minute
I composed myself, and then open the door slowly
And to my surprise, you were at the door
What a wonderful way to trick me at 3p.m.
Now, let's go pick up where we left off
Let's make some stimulating, wild and nasty love

A Double Scoop

A double scoop of French Vanilla with a strawberry swirl
That was the flavor of the Ice cream cone he ordered
I watched him as he enthusiastically grabbed the cone
From the cashier's hand
His eyes were so bright as they lit up opened wide
And his expression of joy was like that of a 10 year old
boy

I pleasantly smiled as he licked the sides of the
Double scoop of vanilla with strawberry
Swirls in the middle
Then suddenly I couldn't take my eyes off him
The way he was eating that ice cream cone
Made me wish that I was the one sitting on top of that
Cone with my legs spread wide, my wetness dripping
His tongue licking, swirling, pulsating
The way he dove into that ice cream made me hot

He licked it with so much care and intensity,
That I became envious of that lucky ass ice cream cone
He was not going to give up until the ice cream gave in
Until there was no more wetness dripping off the
Sides of the cone
Nothing more to taste – just the squirts of uh-ah, oh
baby! Yes! Lick my vanilla until it's gone

Then you will find a strawberry swirl in the middle
That's right, lick your fingers; stick them deep inside me
Let my ice cream spread all over your face
Then I'll kiss it, and lick, and lick,
And kiss it off of your lips
I watched a stranger lick an ice cream cone
And I wished that it was me.....ummmm

A First Kiss

I see, I want, I desire
I feel, absorb, and entertain the thought
Of what it would be like if you desired me as I desire
you

If our lips met in the same room, lying on the same bed,
Sharing the same tongue
How many bolts of energy would shoot down my back
bone?
How many fingernail marks would be embedded in your
Back because you felt so good, that I could not let you
go?
How many lite nibbles would I impress upon your neck
Before kissing your wet lips again

I thirst for your touch
I thirst for your kiss
I thirst for the opportunity to love you
I am hot like the desert, and you quench my thirst
Like water

I see, I want, I desire
How many days will go by before we share a first kiss?
I know you want to, I see it in your eyes

My lips are your lips
My touch is your touch
Especially when I am alone
As I touch myself it is as if you are touching me
Kissing me, caressing me
I want you to want me back
I want you to kiss me
So, that we can experience the mystery of a first kiss

A Pleasure To Know

You are picture perfect fine
Smooth as a glass of the best red wine
You represent the salt of the earth
Your taste is as delightful as my favorite dessert

Knowing you is a special treat
Yes, I'll take a break so we can meet
I'm never too busy to be in your presence
Because our exchange is sensuously pleasant

When you speak, you voice tones are high tidal waves,
Low bass drums
And seductively intoxicating like coconut rum

Your body language moves, grooves, and soothes my
soul
As my body interprets every line and filling every hole
Bridging every gap to make sure time is well spent
Blending, loving, kissing, sipping, laughing, dancing –
Heaven sent

Your mind is just as beautiful as your seductive lure
You are compassionate, confident,
And a great entrepreneur
This is why I don't hesitate to be by your side
In the presence of a true man, my feelings I cannot hide

You are my teacher, my leader, my companion,
And my lover
We will grow together and leave nothing uncovered
Yes, the world should know about you and me
Happiness in contagious and true love will set us free

Only you could inspire me to write these words
From my heart
My admiration and respect for you should never be left

Unspoken not even in the dark

You are indeed, a pleasure to know

All In One Look

As we walked towards each other
Our eyes met, and all in one look
My body is filled with warmth and passion
I feel your eyelashes caress my face moving
Up and down then your eyes find my lips
Ooh...your lips are so soft and uhm so gentle

Then your eyes work down to my neck
Without saying a word, they slowly touch my breasts
I feel a kiss on my navel
Your tongue tasting me like a lollipop
Then, your nose goes deep into my vagina
Just to get a wiff of my sweet smelling pus-sona

Your passion works its way up to my eyes again
I can feel the way you want me
I know that look – piercing, yet with a charming boyish
Blush, you can tell that I want you too
I cannot break our eye contact for I am intrigued
When you look at me, my mind begins to welcome
Every one of your naughty thoughts
And with pleasure I look at you with mutual desire

It's just a matter of time before one of us opens the
door Into the inevitable
At that moment, you smile and say, "Hello"
But I dare not say a word, I am paralyzed
For I am taken by the fullness of your lips and the smell
of Your spicy cologne
I can only part my lips with amazement and
acknowledge You with a nod as you slowly brush by
I take in the sensuous stimulations then exhale -aahh
Oh what lusty quivers my body felt, all in one look

Between My Golden Arches

Between my golden arches lie all of the answers
To life's mysteries
Like, where did I come from?
What is my purpose?
And, who gets to play with the gold between my
arches?

Between my golden arches lie all of the answers
To your questions to make your life easier
Like, how do I relieve my frustration?
What do I do with all of this energy?
And, who gets to play with the gold between my
arches?

My golden arches do not mean the arches of my breast
Or the arch of my back, or the arches that makes
The 'M' shape of my ass
My golden arches do not represent fast food, drive thru,
Or a quick meal while you're on the go. I am a sit down,
Take your time, four course meal at a five star
restaurant.

My golden arches should not go unnoticed;
They desire security, affection, and true love
My golden arches should get lots of attention,
They desire touching, rubbing, squeezing.....and love

My golden arches mean attraction, interest, desire,
teasing, Nibbling....
My golden arches mean excitement, exploring,
touching,

Kissing, sucking...

Cuddling, talking, laughing...
Rubbing, grinding, poking around ...

Feeling, expressing, longing...
Heavy breathing, intensity, wild...

Passion, burning, fire...
Straddling, missionary, sideways, downward dog!

Did I say downward dog? Yes you did

Spanking, biting, restraint, no restraints, climax,
ahhhhh!

Back breaking, earth shaking, love making, finger lickin'
Good kind of man - I think I struck gold
Full lips, tight grip, wide hips, at my finger tips kind of
Woman - I know I struck gold

Between my golden arches lies a valuable treasure
Between my golden arches lies an abundant amount of
Valuable jewels

Bees come from afar for this honey, but not everyone
gets To drink the nectar from between my golden
arches

Chocolate Cognac Kisses

The Ritz Carlton lounge, 24th floor, we sit comfortably
With a view overlooking the city
The lounge is full of people tonight, but somehow we
Convince ourselves that we are here alone

We share a glass of cognac and rich chocolate –
Melted with the desire to mix flavors with a kiss
You sip the cognac while I wear the melted chocolate
On my lips
We exchange flavors of bitter sweet tongue
Licking delicious surprises

The warmth of your lips from the cognac is a passionate
Heated delight of joy as they press against mine
I open up willingly as you deposit the cognac
Into my mouth
Then you seductively lick the melted chocolate
From my lips

Yummy, you taste so intoxicating
My head is spinning, I don't know if I'm tipsy
From the cognac or your kisses
You are so inviting drawing me into you
I'd be foolish to pass up this invite – I must accept
I want to stay awhile and do it until I am satisfied –
Satisfied with melted chocolate cognac kisses

Each time you sip the smooth soothing cognac,
I make sure my lips are covered like chocolate lipstick
Our bodies are slowly moving closer by the inch
That's right; come closer to wet your sexy appetite
So that our kisses are deeper than the ones before

Now it's my turn to sip the cognac and give it to

You mouth to mouth
And your turn to wear the melted chocolate
So I can suck it off your lips
The exchange of flavors will be umm....you know
Dark, tangy, juicy, sweet, sensuously succulent
successfully Swapped swished and then swallowed

I don't care who can see that I am turned on by you
I don't care who knows that I am going
Home with you to finish what we started
I don't care who sees me ravishing in your kisses as if
I went to another dimension in time and space

Our chemistry is like an out of body experience
Where I am watching you seduce me with a
Glass of cognac and melted chocolate
My body travels to the future – to a place where
We are making love
I must come back to the present to carry out our
destiny
Now I understand how we convinced each other
That we were alone in that crowded lounge
No one else mattered, because to us, they did not exist

No, I am not strange –
You are just that damn good, excitingly sensuous
And delicious
I will always remember the night we shared
Coco-Cognac-O-Holic Kisses

Cozy

Comfort, comfy, cozy
So intimate and enclosed
It is the coziness I feel with you with or without clothes
We fit together like paper comes from trees
So warm with hot moments and lots of steam

We cuddle at night just like two spoons
And we sleep until the clock hits noon
Often we seem as if we are one person
A true extension of self
Knowing our cozy time cannot be duplicated
With anyone else

I especially like it when we duck under the covers
We play and wrestle, we kiss and bite
We act like newly found lovers
You're like a big body pillow
You're such a joy to lay with
You are so freakin' hot – when you're on top
You feel like an electric blanket

Warm and comfy, cozy and snugged
A great way to end and start the day
With one of your fabulous hugs

Ditto

I love being with you, talking to you
When I see you, my heart jumps out of my chest
And don't want to come back
But I play it cool because I don't want you to know
That you drive me crazy

Then you said...Ditto

My blood pressure elevates
My pupils dilate, my mouth salivates as I anticipate
Feeling your masculine arms wrapped around
My curvaceous body
Uhm, you have the best touch
When I don't see you I miss you so much

Ditto

I love it when you look into my eyes
Rub my back, feel my thighs
Kiss my neck

Your rich voice, and your genuine smile
Makes me hungry for your nourishment
Thirsty for your sweat
Ready to dive into your dessert
With my cherries on top

Can't you see what's happening?
I'm feeling you deeply
Do you feel the same for me?

You said, Ditto, Ditto

At last, I found you – my love has come along
At last, a beautiful man who is now my favorite my song
I need you in my life
I want you to share my life

And I love you for the rest of my life

And you said...Ditto

Give Me 1 Hour

Give me 1 hour with you
That will be all I need to please
Every inch of your soft beautiful skin
I will start by kissing your toes
Oh I love your pretty toes
Always smooth and nicely polished
In bright sexy colors

I can make a tingling sensation
Flow from your toes up your spine
Every time I use my tongue to lick between
While gently sucking your toes

My lips make their way up to
Your petite sexy ankles
They are in need of my immediate attention
My kisses are for your entire body
Uhm moah

As I move up to kiss your legs
I rub your thighs and tease your big round ass
With the tips of my fingers
Just relax and close your eyes
Enjoy the ride my tongue has prepared for you

I continue to tickle your inner thighs
I can tell you like that
Because you grab the back of my head
And try to guide me to kiss between your legs
Be patient my love, you will get every part of your
Body kissed and more

Just give me 1 hour
And I'll give you a world of
Quivering, earth moving orgasms
Uhm moah.....oh yeah
That's the scream I've been waiting for

As you quiver with chills of escalated passion
I will playfully wiggle my tongue along your navel
Then up to your...
Oh my dear love, you have the sweetest tasting breasts!
I think I'll stay here for a moment, for I must give both
of them equal affection

Time to turn over on your stomach so that I can
Sensually caress your back with my wet kisses
As I rub my body against yours to reach
And suckle your neck
I know you can feel my hardness loving the feeling
Of your roundness
You turn to willingly to give me your lips
You are wet, wild and ready for me to enter inside
But my hour is up....to be continued

Got Ass?

An ass that's symmetrical is pleasing to the eye
Walking, jogging, or dancing it has the ability to
hypnotize
Whether it's hidden in some boxers, or in a visible thong
Ass hoisted in the air clapping to your favorite song

A round toned ass is what a man wants
A jiggly, flabby, fat ass will make him go soft
A big, firm, hot ass will make him co-owner
He will wear it out like a pair of ass-otoners

Ass-symmetrical, is a round tear drop heart shaped ass
Ass-tronomical, is an inconceivably large, yet nice ass
Ass-trology, is the study of staring at the ass
Ass-tonishing, is a surprising discovery of a fabulous ass

The Ass is the stimulator, and the money maker
The arouser, the activator, and the love maker
From the tiny waist line, to the contour of the onion
To the wiggle, and the torque that keeps you crying

Everyone needs an ass to behold
Its beauty and plumpness never gets old
Some of us have it, and while others go and buy it
You will fall in love the first time you try it

It's sleek, dynamic curves protrudes a mile away
It's magical
Proportional with shape, depth, and weight
It's Ass-symmetrical

Got Ass?

Hugs and Kisses

This is a hugs and kisses poem
Written especially for bedtime
Promise to read it each night before falling asleep...
As needed
I want to give you a big hug
When I hug you, will I get the chance to hold you?
I long to feel your chest pressed against mine
I want to listen to your heart beat, feel your warmth,
And experience the strength in your arms
Wrapped around my body
I want to connect the dots, close the gap
And build a bridge from my heart to yours
No trespassers, no solicitors
Only authorized personnel can enter

Can you feel me when you hug me?
Yes you can hold me – as long as you like
Feel the softness of my skin
My tender caress that massages your back
And then squeezes it tight
As if my whole being is wrapped around
You for the moment
Enjoy the sensuality of my touch
And listen to the rhythm of my heart beat
When it touches yours
I never thought that a hug can be so satisfying,
So appetizing, so gratifying
So filled with everything I always wanted to say,

Conveying those thoughts of everything
I always wanted to do
Experience this hug before you go to sleep and you will
surely wake up with a smile on your face

Are you ready for the kisses poem?
Are you ready to feel the soft cushion of the
Fullness of my lips?
They are gentle, and loving if you want them to be
They are passionate, and sensual if you want them to be
They can be joined with yours, if you want them to be
My lips can be a friend, or they can be much
More than a friend
My lips can know your lips, your neck, your ears,
Your navel
My lips can know your body very well
My lips can bring you comfort, happiness, and release
My lips may be the answer to your prayer
So, hugs and kisses at bedtime to enhance your smile
For a brighter day, and a much more fulfilling night
Hugs and kisses to you, and me
Something you must experience….
Much better than a dream
So, this hug is for you, and this kiss is on me☺

I Like The Way I Taste
(When It Is Mixed With Your Saliva)

You made love to my body
Like living waters flowing through a desert place
Caressing and kissing as our sweat drenched the sheets
As we found peace in a heated embrace

Kissing me from my lips down to my toes and up
To my inner thighs
Kiss me just two inches higher
So you will find a wet surprise

Uhmm, yeah that's it - your tongue so precise,
Your mouth so hot
That my back begins to arch and my hips move
Back and forth
As your tongue dances around my spot

I'm about to cum, as the intensity grows
I grab your head to make you go faster
Then my body contracts and I let it go – Ahh!

My juices dripping from your lips like hot lava
You put your tongue deep into my mouth
Wow, I like the way I taste
When it's mixed with your saliva

The taste was very subtle with a hint of spicy wetness
Your lips had a sweet aroma that invited me to explore
As I tasted my own wet, sensuously sweet essence

Uhmm, I like the way I taste
When it is mixed with your saliva

I MISS ALL OF YOU

My man asked me, "Do you miss me, baby?" I said very
lovingly, "You just want to hear me say it.
You know I miss you." He said, "What do you miss?"

Well baby, I miss your smile, your teeth, your lips
I miss your shoulders, your knees, and your fingertips
I miss your eyebrows
And all the little things you do to make me say 'wow'
I miss your socks, your shirt and your toothbrush
I miss your back, your elbows, and your collarbone
Your liver, spleen, and kidneys

See baby, I miss all of you

I miss your warm heart and your healing touch
I miss the love we make, and our bond of trust
I miss kissing your neck, lips, and stomach
And every unmentionable place that feel so right
I miss our screams of passion in the middle of the night
I miss your eyes beaming into mine
Your hot breath blowing in my ear

See baby, I miss all of you

I miss your sandals, your tennis shoes, and your cologne
Our amazing conversations of peace and love
When we are alone
I miss your voice, your laugh, and your facial
expressions When you are in deep thought
And the stories you share about your childhood
memories
And your plans for the future, and your political views,
And your compassion for humanity

See baby, I miss all of you

The good, the bad, and the sensual
The funny, the serious, the lovable
The boyish playfulness, the walks
The quality time, the exploration, and relaxation
I know you get the point but I will never cease
To let you know

See baby, I miss all of you
Oh yeah, and I miss your wallet too

ICE

When I think of ice
I think of chilly, refreshing little cubes
Waiting to be heated by the right touch
Rising to the right temperature
Melting down to give a cold splash of relief

Now I place the chilled cube in my mouth
It's so cold, it feels like heat at first
But as the ice gets familiar with my taste
It begins to blend smoothly as it slowly melts
Into a sensuously delightful experience

The ice will grant you any request you desire
But you must be patient
For I must swirl my tongue around until my icy lips
Are ready to perform whatever you require

I swallow what is constantly melting
And let the rest drip down the sides of my mouth
I love to feel the running stream of passion
Imagine, this is only a hint of what I want you to feel
Pure ecstasy, blissful joy, and rapid tingling
Throughout your body

I remove the ice from my mouth
My lips are ready to transfer the tantalizing
Tease of sudden cold to your body
But I will make you wait
Giving you a little here and a little there
Or sometimes none at all

Did I mention you are blindfolded?
Blindfolds and ice always add a bit of mystery
Heightened sensuous expectation, and sexual
adventures Into the deep

Maybe on our next quest,
You can be the taster, the teaser, the icicle pleaser
I would love to be the deserving recipient
Of selfless giving and anticipated mental orgasms
And ice screams in the middle of the night

Ice, ice, baby
Is much more than a below zero hexagonal crystal
The art of ice sculpting your body is in the heat of fusion
That breaks the illusion of the underestimated
Power of... ICE

Intimacy Unspoken

You entered the room no words were spoken. You lie on the bed on your side, I sit beside you. I want to talk about the events of the day but I hesitate to speak, maybe because I can feel your eyes beaming through me intensely.

At first I avoid eye contact, but you are trying to tell me something. I have never seen this side of you; I am not sure what you are telling me. You roll over on your back, just then I decide to leave the room to let you rest. Before I arose you gently pull my arm back to sit on the bed. Then you pull me towards you as you lean in towards me. I thought you would kiss me but you didn't. Instead, you stroked my back and brushed my hair from my face with your fingers and looked at me with a sense of joy. You were touching me very gently and lovingly.

At that moment you kissed me passionately. We were ravishing one another with echoes of moans. I anticipated this kiss, which increased the sexual tension between us.

Suddenly, we were not kissing anymore; we were ripping off each other's clothes. We are now naked; I'm on top of you kissing you. You roll us over so that you are on top of me. You are warm and I can feel all of you touching every part of me.

You began to kiss my neck and worked your way down.

When you got to my navel, you pushed my legs apart. You viewed my vagina like a priceless painting. You said it was so beautiful. As you continued to examine and admire my vagina, my mind slipped into bliss and my heart slowly crumbled. What a delight for me that you admired my mind, body, and spirit.

Then you kissed it with care and precision. My screaming and body trembles let you know how effective your kisses are. As you enter inside me, we make love until the sun rises. You are an unselfish lover, the best suited for my body.

Now I understand that we don't always need to talk to show our appreciation for each other. What a marvelous experience, and may we have many more.

Kissing You

I kissed you like it was my last kiss
Although it felt like my very first
Like a cup filled with passion
Poured into my soul to quench my sensual thirst

Interpretations of your energy spoke to my heart
Yes, your lips were firmly placed on mine
But my heightened senses knew that you
Wanted more of me
I knew that our kisses were speaking a special language
Because I wanted more of you

This type of connection can only happen between lovers
Between a man, and a woman
Between those with a deep hunger to satisfy the other
This connection happened between you and me

I moaned softly, because it was more than I expected
You tasted like a sweet vanilla ice cream cone
On a hot summer day
I couldn't resist licking, swirling my tongue around
The sides, and nibbling your full, irresistible,
Comforting, inviting lips

I moaned constantly, because your lips touched my lips
Your lips felt like hands that rubbed, and grabbed
Like arms, that held me tightly
Like a tongue sucking all the right places
Like an orgasm that never ends

I moaned loudly to shout for joy

Joy of knowing you
Joy of creating and sustaining passion with you
Joy of making love with a simple kiss

Kissing you is like a visit to the Niagara Falls
Ever flowing with different heights, streams,
And levels of intensity
Fascinating to watch, and tempting to jump into
The deep waters of passion, desire, curiosity, affection,
Admiration, respect, and harmony

Kissing you reaffirmed the purpose of a man
All of the fire, tingling sensations, and oils in my body
Rose to the occasion
Because you hold the Yang that will satisfy
And balance my Yin
You have the combination that unlocks my safe
You have the touch that sends electricity into my
channels, And awaken my desire

Kissing you should be a requirement
Every time our eyes meet
And every time my mind dwells on the things
You do to me
We should always kiss even if it is for a
Fraction of a second
Because I have come to know that
A kiss is not a kiss unless
I am Kissing You

Love My ABC's

A is for your Ability to Allure And Attract my Attention And Appeal to my Appetite

B is for 'I have your Back' Baby. In Bed, in the Bath, and Beyond.

C is for when you Call my name before you Climb Crazy off the Chain while Communicating Creative Creations uhmm like Candy.

D is for Destiny. As we Dive head first into Deep Delicious Dark Delicacies of the Devine Design.

E is for the Energetic Electricity Excelling through the Elegance of Erotic Easels of artistry Expressing Everything Effortlessly.

F is for the Fascinating Friendship, Freaky Fun and the Free Flowing Finger licking Foreplay.

G is for your Giving Gracious heart. You are a Gift from God.

H is for the Hearty Hugs and the Huge Heart you Have.

I is for the Incredible, Insatiable, Irresistible ways that you and I Interact.

J is for Just in time, Just the right size, height and Juiciness.

K is for the Kind, cuddly King of my heart.

L is for the Leader of Love and Laughter that Leaps into Lover's Lane.

M is for My Main Man, My Masculine Match.

N is for our Naughty by Nature Nudity, and the Naked Newness of loving you in the Now.

O is for your Optimum performance, your Openness, and Opportunity to Occupy my body.

P is for Pleasing my Private Parts in Perfect Proportions. Proposing a Place for Physical Peace.

Q is for the Quiet Quality time spent.

R is for the way you Relieve me, and the way I Receive you and give you Release.

S is for Sensuality. A Sudsy bath, a Sexy dace, and a Sweet Succulent Song.

T is for your Touch. Tantalizing, Tender, Teasing, Tickling, and Tight.

U is for you can stand Under my Umbrella because you are Unique and Unbelievably Understanding.

V is for the Voluptuous curves you Venture Valiantly, Very satisfying, and Very addicting.

W is for your Witty Words of Wisdom, and the Way you Wet my Whistle While Whisking me away.

X is for your X-ray transparency making it possible to see right into your eXtremely eXtraordinary heart.

Y is for YOU. I could not have asked for anyone better than YOU.

Z is for Zero. Zero represents the number of times that you will be refused when it comes to making love.

Now you know why I love my ABC's
Tell me what you think of me

Magic Lips

The woman with magic lips
Need no hips
To persuade his magic wand to arise
No abra-ca-dabra, or hocus pocus
Nor is there a hidden surprise

Just her natural ability to make sounds and rhythms
Enough to move him to join the dance
No clothing needs to be removed
Or any fantasies to prove
Just her magic lips and her hands

He has the water and the pot
She has the fire
As they get heated up
Steam is what is inspired

He releases his steam with a scream
Yet she doesn't stop right there
His body shakes and squirms
His mind has nowhere to turn
But his eyes gaze upon her with flare

"How did you do that?"
Is all he could sigh
She swallowed and then replied

"I have magic lips
That sways like hips
With a most convincing grip
That takes you on a trip

How soon you forget
The lips that kiss
Because the lips becomes anything you wish"

Oh what a feeling
When the lips are willing
To him it's a spell
But the magic lips
Never tell

Medieval Good Times

I have a craving for dessert and for you
Let's mix them together to see how they taste
Medieval madness ice cream with caramel sauce
Drizzled on top
That is what I want smudge all over your hot naked
body

No worries about it being too cold
When the ice cold meets your heated body
The ice cream will melt creating a delightful feeling
You will not be able to constrain yourself, especially
when I begin to lick it off
I will start any where you want me to...anywhere

No bowls, no spoons, no napkins
Just your body and my tongue
Lots of fun, laughter, moans, and groans
Ooos and aahs, and slurps and swallows
We will have a medieval good time

My Lover

I don't usually do this, but...

My name is Honey
I want you to be my special friend
I believe we can make each other feel good
Where do you want to go?
It's not important where we go
I just want to be with you, o.k.?

I don't usually do this, but...

You are an exception
Let's talk about it over dinner
And eat each other for dessert
How do you want to be served?
I will be your cherry pie a la mode
And you will be my banana daiquiri

I don't usually say this, but...

I want you to be my lover
I want to be your lover
What can I do for you?
You are very sexy, and sensual
I desire to kiss your lips
The lust in me desires to touch you
Please make love to me

You are my lover
I am your lover
Let's go do the things that lovers do
I can't wait any longer
For you are my only lover

My Tribute To Men

Black-the color of your skin enriched with chocolate sun rays drizzled with the radiance of morning dew

Brown- the color of your locks, the earth's tone, the song of nature, the bronze highlights of the sunset; so pure, so curly, so unique

Dark Red-the color of your lips, sweet as cherries, a succulent surprise when they are met with mine, the taste of red wine blended with perfection to be sipped slowly to enjoy the flavor

Red- the color of your body heat, together our friction burns deep into the core of the earth creating a fire, towering like a volcano hot enough to erupt, waiting to spill your lava into the earth's tunnels of love. The ascension of hot steaming passion reaches its zenith, then ahh!

Orange-the color of your flavor, you sweet, tangy, fine fruit of nature-you, your body sweat is like citrus juice with tropical undertones and a scoop of protein to make a rich delicious smoothie

Gold-the color of your heart, goodness and sincerity beams from your soul, your value is priceless, timeless, and ageless, and cannot be duplicated-for you are the original man

Green- the color of your eyes, reflecting the tall grass in which you kneel down to focus on your prey, you are the hunter, the gatherer, the provider, and the life line.

Blue-the color of the peace within you, you are able to quiet a storm, and settle the rough ocean, you tame the wild, and causes evil to dissolve in your presence

Violet-the color of your total being, a mixture of strength, passion, sincerity, protection, and peace. These are the colors that capture the essence of who you are. You are to be celebrated, appreciated, and elevated.

So, I welcome the opportunity to taste the rainbow.

Poetry Formerly Known As
(The Beginning)

My *'Darling Nikki'*,

Here's *'The Plan'*: Drive *'Uptown'* to *'Erotic City'* in your *'Lil Red Corvette'*. Meet me at *'3121'* *'Alphabet Street'* on the *'Graffiti Bridge'* by *'Paisley Park'*. *'Get on the Boat'* at *'7'*. *'Do U Lie'*? Tell them your name is *'Lolita'*, and you are the *'Sexy Dancer'* for *'Mr. Happy'*. You don't know the *'Bat Dance'*? Well, *'U Got the Look'*. Tell them you are a *'Friend, Lover, Sister, Mother, Wife'*, or *'Slave'*. It doesn't matter. I will be boarding as *'Mr. Goodnight'*, a.k.a. your *'International Lover'* for the evening.

Go to room *'319'*, the password is *'Elephants and Flowers'*. Look inside the *'Chocolate Box'*, light the *'Incense and Candles'*. Take out the *'Starfish and Coffee'* with *'Cream'*. Put on the *'Pink Cashmere'*, and the *'Raspberry Beret'*. Then, let's make a toast. To *'The Most Beautiful Girl In The World'* *'Nothing Compares 2 U'*. *'If I Was Your Girlfriend'* I would *'Adore'* *'All The Midnights In The World'*, get the *'Rainbow People'* together to make it *'Purple Rain'* for *'A Million Days'*. Cause *'Baby I'm A Star'* on *'Planet Earth'*. *'Party Up'*, *'We Can Funk'*, *'Musicology'* will begin to play. *'When We're Dancing Close and Slow'* I will say, dearly beloved we are gathered here today to get to *'The Sensual Ever After'*. *'I Would Die For You'* by committing *'Sexual Suicide'*, so *'Let's Go Crazy'* in our *'Sexuality'*, *'Girls and Boys'* until we are *'Satisfied'*.

Poetry Formerly Known As
(The Middle)

'When Doves Cry', 'The Beautiful Ones' always 'Play in The Sunshine'. So 'Tell Me How U Wanna Be Done'? I'll give you 'Illusions, Coma, Pimp and Circumstance', 'D.M.S.R', and 'Delirious' 'Temptation'. Just don't make me 'The One U Wanna C', 'Always In My Hair', or try 2 B my 'Future Baby Mama' when 'It' is over. 'The Question Of You' saying things like 'Te Amo Corazon', 'Take Me With You', 'How Come You Don't Call Me Anymore' will only create 'Xenophobia'. That means I will 'Shake' you like a 'Tambourine'. You know, 'Fury', 'Arrogance', a 'Condition Of The Heart'.

Let's get an understanding; we are just '2 Nigs United 4 West Compton' for 'Sex In The Summer'. 'Money Don't Matter 2nite' it's the 'Sign 'O' the Times' in case you haven't noticed. There are 'Thieves in the Temple', 'Something in the Water', and a 'Lady Cab Driver' brought me here. That's a 'Scandalous' 'Controversy' in 'Pop Life', especially when 'All The Critics Love U In New York'.

'I Could Never Take The Place Of Your Man', 'Cinnamon Girl'. But, My 'Love Machine' can 'Do It All Night' 'What Do You Want Me To Do'? 'I Feel For You', 'Eye Wanna Melt With U', 'I Wanna Be Your Lover'. Let's 'Kiss' until we work up a 'Black Sweat'. 'Damn U', I'm 'Rock Hard In A Funky Place', 'Now' Let your 'Dirty Mind' Give me 'Head'. 'Get it Off' like you've never done before. 'New Position', 'Face Down' 'On The Couch'. 'Let Me Lick Your Pussy', I wanna be 'Under the Cherry Moon' so I can 'Jack You Off' while you 'Do Me Baby'. Uhm, you're so 'Soft and Wet', your 'Pheremone' taste like an 'Insatiable' 'Peach'. Don't stop, there's a 'Joy in Repetition', 'Trust'.

Poetry Formerly Known As
(The Conclusion)

Let me find your *'Diamonds and Pearls'* until you *'Tick, Tick, Bang'! 'Another Lover Hole N Yo Head'.*
It's time for *'Le Grind'* I will *'Push'* my *'Thunder'* between your *'Mountains'*, then swirl it into your *'Lemon Crush'*. *'Let's Work'* Yeah, *'Daddy Pop'* it *'Round and Round'*, *'Dead On it'*. *'Get Your Groove On' 'Sister'*. In *'The Screams of Passion' 'Call My Name'*. *'My Name Is Prince'*, you *'Irresistible Bitch'*,

Now its time my *'Computer Blue'* put your *'Endorphin Machine'* on *'Automatic' 'Pussy Control'*. *'Slow Love'*, *'Walk Don't Walk'*, *'Come Back'* into *'The Arms Of Orion' 'Willing and Able'*. *'I Can't Stop This Feeling I Got'*. *'Eye No'* I gotta *'Release It'*. *'1+1+1=3'*, It's time for the big *'Orgasm'*. *'In This Bed Eye Scream'*: *'Glam Slam'*, *'Gold'*, *'Housequake'*, *'Love Sexy'*, *'Jughead'*, *'Sexy Mutha Fucker'*, *'Billy Jack Bitch,' Super Funky Cali Fragi Sexy'*, *'I Hate You' 'Anna Stesia'*, *'And God Created Woman'*, *'Betcha By Golly Wow'*, *'Life Can Be So Nice'*. *'Shhh'*.

Time for *'Resolution'*, *'We Gets Up'*, I wash my *'Lion Of Judah'*. I say thank you for riding *'The Continental'* and going with *'The Flow'*, *'Sometimes It Snows In April'*. There are *'3 Chains Of Gold'* on *'My Computer'*, take it. Then, I set *'Cindy C.'*, *'Bambi'*, *'Melody Cool'*, or whatever her name was, *'Free'*. Don't be *'So Blue'*, *'Let It Go'*. This is *'America'*. *'Dance On'*, go *'Sleep Around'*, *'Hot Thing'*. I gotta be *'Around The World In A Day.'* It's time for my *'Guitar' 'Solo'* for *'Anne Christian'*, and the *'Pope'...'Welcome To The Dawn'*.

Safe Word

Hey honey, let's play a game
Remember how we talked about the blindfolds?
Well, I've given it some thought, and I'd like to try it
But first, we must come up with a safe word

Yes, a safe word – just in case I do something over the top
And you want me to slow down or stop
It has to be a simple off topic word
Something that could break my concentration

How about Superman? No, if I'm lost in the moment
I may think you are calling out my name because
You're in pure ecstasy

Chandelier – that's too kinky, I'm gonna think you want
to Go for a swing. Hmm, I wonder if our chandelier can
Support both of us... anyway, make a mental note to
self For another day

Coffee cakes – that will only inspire me to spank dat ass
T-Rex – nah, that is gonna make me go buck wild and
Primal on your ass while we're making love

Hey, I got one. How about 'red light'?
You know like the game that kids play
Green light means, keep it coming
Yellow light means, slow down you're going too fast
And red light means, stop...that's the safe word, red light
You like it? Good. Let's play....Green light –

Twinkies & Strawberry Sauce

Oh he was a big fat playa but with a lot of swag
He had a round boyish face with a chin that sagged
His wide large body resembled a beer keg
And was disproportionate to his long slim legs
His suit was too big, and his cologne too strong
With someone like me, he could never get it on
He wasn't quite the size to fit my appetite
But something in his eyes felt quite right
He took me off guard, especially when he said
I would be his
I laughed it off and thought to myself,
"Not in a million years"
He had a lot of confidence and the gift of
Persuasion on his side
As he walked away I had a feeling of loss on my mind
That clever bastard, how could this be?
He's suppose to be runnin' after me
But let me tell you what this big fat playa did to me

Twas the night before Christmas not a soul on the street
He asked me to his limo, and I took a seat
Are you hungry? Yes I am. Not a restaurant open
So we sat in the limo laughin' and jokin'
Our eyes met, and so did our lips
I soon forgot he had the bigger hips
It was something about him that sparked my attraction
It wasn't his looks, perhaps it was his actions
I wanted him bad, and he could tell
He pulled out his twinkie, and my jaw nearly fell
He put it in my mouth, and I smeared it all over his face
Then with a kiss, I let him have a taste
He found the strawberry sauce and without a word

We knew to devour the desert being served
We took a passionate pause then striped off our clothes
In the back of the limo, anything goes
He made me feel sexier than ever and
I didn't want to let him down
He was too big to straddled so we let creativity abound
We seduced our sensual hunger by allowing
Food to be the boss
Then he dipped his twinkie in my strawberry sauce
My body turned into a platter for passionate pleasure
We fed one another, played and teased
That moment was definitely a night to treasure

"Will I see you again?" I said with a smile
He said, "You see me now", and I nearly went wild
I jumped back in the limo, we went to his house
I loved his twinkies, and he loved my strawberry sauce
Food and sex worked well for us
And now I love every acre of my big fat playa
Who would've thought?

What I Am

I am the alpha and the omega
I am the bedroom, the bed, the sheets, and the pillow
I am hard when you want it rough
And I am soft when you need a woman's touch

So, fuck the best of both worlds
When you are with me, you get the whole galaxy
I am the sun that keeps you hot
The stars you shoot for when you cum

I am not just a woman, but better than a woman
Because I can give you everything you need…
And I mean every got dam thing!
So, you can take the blue pill, and walk out the door
Or you can take the red pill and have the time of your
life

Now, I'm going to pour myself a drink and
Go into my bedroom
You have 10 seconds to decide what you want to do
The blue pill, which is out the door
Or the red pill which is the door to my galaxy

PAMELA NORRIS

Who Are You?

Who are you?

Entering my space, changing my flow?
You took my soul to a place I've never known

I was buried in my work – no time to come up for air
Somehow out of nowhere you appeared there

Tall, fine, and lovely
Warm to the touch, soft to my lips
Sensuality shared for the first time

Wow, feels like Christmas in the spring
Inspiration in a storm

Who are you?

Able to get my attention
Skip knowing your name going right into who you are
Celebrating your being intermixing with mine

Who are you?

I say...
And please come again

You May Use Me Not

You may sweet talk me
While staring into my eyes
You may touch me
Or hug me by surprise
You may adore me, treasure me, or
Love me out of my mind
But you may use me not

Instead, let's look at it as sharing what is true and real
Let's share our needs, desires, and how we really feel
Let's not deny each other from what we naturally find
Let's share more than a moment, or even a lifetime
Though I will share all of me and you will share all of
you
You may use me not

We can splash hot oil all over our bodies
Feed each other strawberries dipped in dark chocolate
Pour champagne straight from the bottle on to my
body; Sip it with your lips
Lick it with your tongue; drink it from my navel
Until I nearly cum
But you may use me not

We can share a wet dream
Slop it with a drenched mouth
Wipe it with a damped cloth
Exchange a dripping French kiss
You can command my lips to do all sorts of tricks
Command my hips to move clockwise, counter
clockwise, Up, down, round and round
But you may use me not

We can read each others' minds
While our hearts connect and get lost as they intertwine
We can fall in love
We can wrestle in the mud,
Or rub each other down with honey, caramel, or fudge
I can be your sexy, cool lover and
Most trusted friend 'til the end
But you may use me not

That way we keep our spiritual energy flowing, our
Physical bodies going, and our mental intellect knowing
As the evidence of our relationship is constantly
Reaping and sowing
Through good times, or bad times, through lots of
money And lots of honey
Through living out our sexual fantasies,
To a quickie at your office – yes please
Remember, we can do this, that, them, and those
But you may use me not

Before we start this romance, we must ask ourselves:
What am I giving? What am I getting?

And the answer must be: Increase and Balance in a
Reciprocated Fashion
With words like caring, loving, and giving
To drive and sustain our passion
Now that we have an understanding of
What we need, want and desire
With an undeniable attraction that transcends
Into a mutha burnin' fire
There is one more thing that must transpire
YOU MAY USE ME NOT

ABOUT THE AUTHOR
The Artist

I am an artist
I paint pictures in your mind
Take your imagination for a ride
Together we sing, dance, laugh, or cry
You can join me on this journey
As I stimulate, educate, and transform
Into this masterpiece created just for you

Let me tap into your soul
Elevate your creative mind as I intertwine
My fantasy with your reality
Through transitions of emotions
Through transitions of different persons, places, or
things
When you step into my world
Jump on board, buckle up, close your mouth,
And open your mind

No need for passenger drivers-just relax
You may judge, you may think, you may join
I, the artist, will drive
I will accelerate, stop, or move this vehicle
You are invited to simply enjoy the ride

Do these masterpieces represent who I am?
Of course not,
Yet it encompasses every essence of my being
My observations, my experiences, and ultimately
My interpretation
It is all of who I am...
The Artist

PAMELA NORRIS

Books By Pamela Norris

- ♥ The Good, The Bad, and The Sensuous

- ♥ Bedtime Poetry: A Sensual Collection

- ♥ To Know Love: The Journey of Giving and Receiving Love

To order additional copies:
- http://www.createspace.com/4622989
- Amazon.com
- Pamela-Norris.com

Contact Information

Email: Artsypoetry101@gmail.com